Thomas Hervey

A Letter from the Honourable Thomas Hervey to the Late King

Thomas Hervey

A Letter from the Honourable Thomas Hervey to the Late King

ISBN/EAN: 9783337195823

Printed in Europe, USA, Canada, Australia, Japan

Cover: Foto ©ninafisch / pixelio.de

More available books at **www.hansebooks.com**

A

LETTER

FROM THE

Hon. THOMAS HERVEY

TO THE

LATE KING.

To which is prefixed one to the

Duke of *NEWCASTLE*,

Recommending the Contents of it to his
GRACE's Furtherance and Favour.

Litteras ab amico miſſas in medium protulit, palamque recita-
vit. Quid hoc eſt, quam tollere e vitâ vitæ ſocietatem ?
CIC. Orat. Phil. II.

LONDON:

Printed for G. WOODFALL, the Corner of *Craig's-*
Court, Charing-Croſs. MDCCLXIII.

[Price One Shilling.]

THE

A U T H O R

TO THE

R E A D E R.

AT the Time of writing this Letter to the King, I little thought of being myself the Publisher of it. On the contrary, in a valedictory one to my Son, when I had the *utmost* Reason to think my End approaching; I desired him to consult two Gentlemen therein mentioned, about the Means of getting it conveyed to his Majesty. This Circumstance sufficiently testifies,

that

that it was intended for a pofthumous Exhibition. In which cafe, the great perfonage to whom it was addreffed, would probably have thought of the moft exceptionable Parts in it, with lefs Severity: Or, if not, its unhappy Author at leaft, could not have been affected, by any Cenfure that might be paft upon it. I am at prefent entirely aware, that the Contents are not near fo much a Concern of the Public, as a Street-ballad: and yet perfuaded, if I could explain my Motives for troubling them with it, but little blame would be imputed to me. The bafe and contemptuous Ufage I received from the Duke of *Newcaftle* upon this Occafion, furpaffes all Precedent. Had he vouchfafed to give any Anfwer at all, to three Letters I writ him, I would not have taken ill the moft rude and

unkind,

unkind, that his Enmity to me could have fuggefted. The not returning my Letter to the King, is an Offence of a ftill more heinous Nature: But that Breach of Truft is accounted for in the Title-page. I had great Reafon, I confefs, to apprehend the Mortification I met with: becaufe an old and intimate Acquaintance of mine, who was pretty high in Office, told me many Years ago, when we were jointly folliciting another thing; that he feared, the Scorn and Derifion, with which my Brother had taken all Opportunities to treat the Duke's Character, had fo exafperated his Grace, as to give him an Averfion even to my Name and Family*. My previous

Mif-

* The Charge brought againft Lord *Herv.y*, I fear, is undeniable: but fuch a Quarrel cannot be deemed fufficient Caufe for profcribing

all

Mifgivings, however, had not fo thoroughly prepared me for the Conflict, as to affwage either the Anger or Anguifh I lived in, for a long Time after, in confequence of the Slight and Indignity put upon me. I exclaimed now and then at the inhuman Violence, with fome Scope and Petulancy: but am pleafed, upon the whole, that his Grace's Age and Station, reftrained me from any other Refentment of it. And yet, to be grievoufly injured, and at the fame Time prohibited Complaint, is Torture: The worft of all Tortures; for it is to be excruciated mentally. It may fuffice now to fay, that to add Weight to the Depreffed, and make Mirth of Mifery, is a Sort of Cruelty,

all his Relations. And yet the great Cardinal *Richlieu* had an Injuftice of this Sort imputed to him.

that,

that, pungent as I felt it, I had much rather fuffer, than inflict.

To wave this hideous Subject, and rid myfelf of the Pain which will for ever attend the Recollection of it ; I fhall proceed to tell my candid and indulgent Reader, the Caufe that more immediately urged me to commit this Trefpafs on him. When an innocent Perfon has been highly injured in his fame, without a Power of redreffing himfelf, he naturally makes his Appeal to the World, as the moft proper Advocate and Judge, in all fuch Cafes : Becaufe the Opinion of the World, in Effect, *is* Fame. I have fome Hopes, befides, that my Slanderers will find in this melancholly Production, fufficient Evidence to convince them, that, noticed for a Philofopher at one fcore

Years

Years of Age, I was fcarcely fo de-
generated, as to be an idle Libertine
at three.

I received two anonymous Letters
laft Year, which have kept me upon
Tenters ever fince. One of thefe
namelefs Scriblers, exprefles his Dif-
regard of me with becoming Mode-
ration : Allows me to have fome
Share of Underftanding, and therefore flatters himfelf, that I may have
Senfe enough to pay a proper Deference to his. In confequence of which,
he further hopes, to find a fuitable
Alteration in my Sentiments; and
that I, as well as his Client, may re-
fpectively reap the Benefit of the
good Office he meant to do us both.
But my courteous Monitor deceives
himfelf moft egregioufly ; for, of
the two, I had rather take another
Affront

affront from him, than his advice. The Ribaldry of the other, is sharpened by such opprobrious Terms and hints, that standing in the Pillory would not be too great a Penalty for his abuse. To be implacably offended, yet treated as the Offender, is a most insupportable Aggravation of my Wrongs. And could I conceive, that such masked Assailants bore Arms, of any Sort, I would submit to the Means of a Prize-fighter, to vindicate my Reputation; and by Advertisement call them forth, to a more proper Encounter of me. For I have so conducted myself through Life, that I am ready to answer to any thing, any Body, and in any Way.

Having unwarily touched upon the Subject of the Duke of *Newcastle*'s Misbehaviour to me, in the

fore-

foregoing Preface; I find it neceffary to add a fhort Supplement to it :
in. order to obviate any Extenuation,
or Replication, that might be made
on his Behalf, relative to this Matter.
Accordingly, the Reader is to be informed, that near two Years after,
upon fome frefh Inducements thereto,
I renewed my Suit to his Grace, under the Mediation of two powerful
Advocates, whofe Sollicitations I
thought he would not be able to with-
ftand : and I judged a-right. For in
confequence of their Intervention,
I obtained, in a fhort Time, an Offer of two Penfions, in Exchange for
my Employment. But upon difco-
vering, in the Midft of our Treaty,
that the Terms of this Compromife
were neither agreeable to my Wifhes,
or Expectations; and the Penfions,

not

not attainable upon the *Irish* Esta-blishment; I had absolutely, and finally, (as I then thought) refused them. Nevertheless, being urged anew to accept the Offer; as the Apothecary tells *Romeo*, when he is vending his Poison to him, " My Poverty confented, but not my Will."

I am inexpressibly obliged to my two noble Interceffors in this negociation; but the credited Side of his Grace's account with me is never to be cancelled. For it is fcarcely within the reach of human Power, to make Retribution for a wounded Pride, and violated Honour: Which are the Feelings of every Man of Spirit, confcious of an unavenged Affront. My great Miftake in this Affair, was not prefenting my Memorial to the King, in Perfon: Be_

caufe

caufe I am thoroughly convinced, (to ufe a Scripture Phrafe) " that it would have found Favour in his Sight."

To bring together the Whole of this Tranfaction, the fubjoining of my Letter to Mr. *Weft* may not be unacceptable to the Reader. The only Thing I afked, on my own Part, relating to this arduous Matter, was to have fome Memorandum made in the Office, that the Penfions were not given entirely *gratis*, but granted upon a Commutation with the Crown. This Indulgence was neverthelefs refufed me, and in a Manner I thought rather too abrupt and arbitrary.

To

To Mr. W E S T, *Secretary to the* Treafury.

S I R,

YOUNG as I was at the Univerfity, where there was too great an Habit of it, I even then abhorred Difputation. Yet a very unfeigned Love of Truth, makes me diflike to have any thing impofed upon me for Reafon, which is not fo. The Tenure of a Place, and that of a Penfion, with regard to the Power of the Crown to take away either, are unqueftionably indifcriminate. But with regard to the Precarioufnefs of the Poffeffions in other Refpects, they

are

are very diftinguifhable. The Equity
of our King, and likewife of his Mi-
nifters, is fo notorious; that a Man
in this Country has little more Chance
to lofe his Office, than to lofe his
Head, without fome Mifdemeanour.
During the Plenitude of Sir *Robert
Walpole*'s Power, indeed, any politi-
cal Herefy was deemed a mortal Sin,
and the Delinquent fuffered accordingly : But having unfortunately quit-
ted my Seat in Parliament, I might
be lefs orthodox than I really am,
without ever expofing myfelf to any
minifterial Anathema on that Account. Now, Sir, if there be nothing erroneous in this Reafoning; the
Inference is, that a *quam diù fe bene
gefferit*, to an harmlefs and dutiful
Servant of the Crown, is pretty near
equal to a Patent for Life. But this
will not be the Cafe of my poor Sub-
ftitutes,

ftitutes, whofe Equivalent for what I
have relinquifhed, will be fubject to
other Contingencies. Penfions, little Penfions I mean, from the Nature
of them, befpeak fome Degree of
Indigence where they are beftowed;
and, confequently, are fuppofed to be
given to Objects of Compaffion. But
fhould his Majefty die, his Succeffor
may poffibly not fee thofe Objects in
the fame Light, or have others recommended to him to whom he may
chufe to give a Preference: And either
of thefe Things would defeat my friend-
lefs Suitors. Mrs. *Hervey*, befides,
in cafe I fhould furvive the King, will
not be found immediately in that Predicament: which might create a farther demur upon her claim. And the
natural Pretence for afking a Conti-
nuance of the Bounty, not appear-
ing; my Plea for fhewing the equi-
tible

table one, by fuch a Memorandum as
I contended for, becomes the ftronger.
Becaufe by this Means it would be
feen, at once, that the Provifion I had
obtained for my Family, was with a
View only of preventing the future
Want, to which they ftood eventually
expofed at my Demife; and that it
was not a mere Act of Grace: As I
had not only given up, in Confideration of it, the prettieft Employment
in the Kingdom, of its Value, but a
Title to about eight thoufand Pounds;
which was as much due to me, by the
Confeffion of Mr. *Pelham* himfelf,
as any Part of my Salary. I am,

S I R,

your moft obedient,

and humble Servant,

Tho. Hervey.

To his GRACE

The DUKE of NEWCASTLE.

MY LORD,

THE inclofed Letter to the King, was
written near four Years ago, upon
an Alarm given me by a Fit of an Apo-
plexy, and an Apprehenfion that my Death
was not far off : Yet I had not the Refolution at laft to deliver it. For I have fuffered, and could ftill fuffer myfelf, to be
much troubled, rather than be a little troublefome. That I am not impofing upon
your Grace in this Affertion, I will give
you the Teftimony of Sir *Robert Walpole*
for my Voucher : Who never made me any
other Excufe for his repeated Neglects and
Abufes of me, than my *being a bad Sollicitor,
and too modeft a Man for public Life*. This
Subterfuge appeared to me fo very mean and
unnatural, that inftead of extenuating the
paft, it gave me frefh caufe of Offence : And
in confequence of the Mortification and
Difguft created by it, I determined foon

B   after

after to quit my Seat in Parliament. Had I
ever attached myfelf to your Grace, I am
perfuaded, that my fervices had come doubly
recommended to you, by fuch a· confideration. But Sir *Robert* unhappily verified a
Sentiment of fome *French* Hiftorian I have
read ; who, in clofing his Remarks upon
Ptolemy's Behaviour to *Pompey*, obferves,
" *Que la Reconnoiffance n'etoit jamais la Vertu*
" *des Grands.*" I have neither Time, nor
Spirits fufficient at prefent, to tell your
Grace, how highly aggravated his mifufage
of me was, from various Circumftances.
Amongft others, my poor weak and paffionate Mother difinherited me, in confequence
of my Compliance with his laft Requeft to
me, in behalf of my Colleague Colonel *Norton :* to whom, I cannot but confefs, that
fhe had a very well grounded Quarrel.
This Schifm amongft ourfelves, was attended with a much greater in the Corporation
of *Bury :* Infomuch, that I found it extremely difficult laft Year, to lay a-new the
Foundation of the *Ickworth* Intereft there.
The bafe, and, I may fay, cruel Part my
Brother *Felton* acted in the Beginning of that
Strife, makes him a Reproach to Human-
Nature.

Nature. But my whole Family, I thank
Heaven, thought fo fuitably of his Behaviour,
that they have all renounced him. I have
mentioned fome of thefe Things in my
Letter to his Majefty : And am giving your
Grace this Trouble, to beg the Favour of
you, not only to deliver it for me, but to
back the humble Suit I have made to him.
Should you fucceed in your good Offices, I
fhall be more beholden to you, than ever I
have been to any other Man in all my
Life. I am,

My Lord,

Your Grace's moft obedient,

Bond-Street.   and humble Servant,

Tho. Hervey.

As I am folliciting the firft, and, in all
probability, the laft Favor I fhall ever afk of
your Grace ; I hope you will pardon me, if
I trefpafs a little longer on your Time and
Patience, by befeeching you farther to make
known to his Majefty, what I am about to
tell you. Mr. *Johnfon*, in writing Mr. *Sa-
vage*'s life, makes the Account of his Mif-
fortunes extremely interefting. And yet,

C 2

were

were I to trouble the World with an Hiftory of mine, how greatly would they be thought to furpafs them? Adverfity feemed to take an early liking to me, as the Perfon, of all Man-kind, moft liable to the dire Effects of it: And it has purfued me with a very invariable Attachment. I loft a Son the laft Campaign in *America*,* almoft as dear to me as my Eye-fight, or any other of my Senfes. And I pro-teft to you, it has made fo horrid an Impref-fion upon my Mind, that I am in fome doubt, whether it would not have been better for me to have loft the Senfes themfelves, 'ere I miffed fo very pleafing an Object of them. Perdition on the Head of him, or rather head-lefs him, that robbed me of it. If he had fallen by any common Chance of War, where he might have done himfelf fome Honour, or the Nation any Service ; I might have fecretly fighed, but could not have re-pined at it. But to be told, that he was a Victim, facrificed to the Mifconduct of his ignorant Leader; and only became a Part of the bloody Oblation made by him to our Enemies ; is an Affliction, which, if it do not prove Mortal, a feeling Perfon may rea-fonably wifh to be fo. There was not a more

* This horrid Difafter happened at *Ticonderoga*.

pro-

promifing young Man in the World. He had all the Spirit, Diligence, and Alacrity, of Lord *Howe* : And I am not fure, that he had not rather the Advantage of him, in point of Parts and Erudition. When I could but ill afford it, I gave him an extraordinary Education, becaufe I could give him nothing elfe: And he had Senfe enough to know, and to reap the Benefit of it. He took an early Liking to his Profeffion, as an Art; and redoubled his Application to it, as a Matter of Duty. There are few Books of any Authority or Repute, which treated of the military Sciences, that he had not read. As this Difpofition could not fail to advance him in Knowledge, his Advancement in Knowledge had likewife procured him fome Confideration and Preferment in the Army. General *Shirley* made him his Aid de Camp, when he was but a Lieutenant: which, I have been told, is not a common Mark of Favor and Diftinction. When he got his Company, he was appointed to the fame Office under Mr. *Webb* ; who was as kind to him, (I thank him) as if he had been his Child. But being difpoffeffed at laft of his little Attainments, and called again into the Ranks;

one

one ill-fated Hour, deprived *him* of his Life,
and me of the Hopes with which I had flattered myfelf, of feeing fome pleafing, ufeful
Sup rftructure raifed, upon the Foundation
we had jointly laid, of a brave, a virtuous,
and fubftantial Man.

Upon my Word, my Lord, I have not
been impofing on you a fictitious Merit,
either created, or even magnified at all,
by my Partiallity as a Parent; but giving
you the genuine Character of a very amiable
and deferving young Perfon. Were I capa-
ble of being blinded by fuch a Prejudice,
the fame Prepoffeffion would make me think
alike of all my Children: but that is not
the Cafe. I have been fatisfied in general,
not to have difcovered any material Defects
in my Offspring: But Content and Admiration are different Things. This unfortu-
nate Youth having poffeffed himfelf of thofe
Things, which throughout the whole Courfe
of my Life, I have made the chief Objects
of my Efteem; he was confequently in Poffeffion of the Efteem itfelf: and I had be-
gun to love him, by a Sort of Obligation
derived from Principle. The natural Relation betwixt us, was improved into a more

in-

intimate and cordial Union ; that of Friend-
ſhip. I do not much affect, or deal in Me-
taphor; but I honour every man, if I may
be allowed the Expreſſion, who is his own
Maker. My Meaning is, that Nature having done her Work, there is a kind of ſe-
cond Formation of the Man, which depends
upon ourſelves : and my poor Boy had made
a Progreſs in that Taſk, very rarely attained
at ſuch an age. But I will dwell no longer
upon the Subject ; for I have really felt new
Anguiſh, from my own Reflections. It will
be no improper Concluſion, however, of this
melancholy Diſcourſe, to tell your Grace,
I moſt heartily wiſh the Sentiments of a
Father were better known to *you*, and that
I had been leſs acquainted with them.

The following Letter is to His Majeſty.

Moſt

Moſt gracious Sir,

IF to have long loved and ſerved You, be any Excuſe for troubling You, or any Title to your Regard; Your Majeſty will not be offended at this Obtruſion on your Thoughts, and more important Callings. And my Attachment to your ſacred Perſon, has not been the leſs firm or faithful, becauſe the Malice of my Fortune has placed me at a greater Diſtance from it than I might have been; or leſs meritorious, becauſe my *Power* of ſerving you may have been more ſcanty and confined, than that of other Men. Whenever Occaſion offered, ſuch Abilities and Means as I was Maſter of, have never failed to be exerted by me, in ſupport of your Majeſty's Government, and in promoting your private Eaſe and Tranquillity. I can farther aver, that for many Years paſt, I never heard of any thing, which I thought might vex or mortify you, without grieving; or any thing which I thought would pleaſe you, that I did not cordially rejoice at it. Yet with all this conſciouſneſs about me, with all theſe Extenuations of my Treſpaſs, I ſhould have been cautious, at a time like this of mentioning to you a private concern

of

of mine, were not the Motives to it too preffing, to be any longer refifted.

My Conftitution, long fince impaired by early Grief and Difappointment, has lately had a Shock, which feems to threaten a total Diffolution of it. Weak and diftempered bodies, I know, are fometimes troubled with fuch Mifgivings, through Fear : but I have not the leaft Reafon to believe, that I am under any Apprehenfion fo created. For though it may be a Queftion, whether I am duely prepared to give that Account of my Life, which I have been told will be required of me ; I am certain at leaft, that no Sage, or Saint, ever felt a more thorough Indifference about the Refignation of it. And yet, notwithftanding the Firmnefs and Compofure, with which I can behold my own, and the End of all Things ; I am difquieted, at Times, with a very painful Anxiety concerning the Means of arriving at it : And perceive myfelf fufpended, in fome fort, by the Dilemma of the Philofopher, who faid he wifhed himfelf dead, but did not like dying.   * This Paradox, if I remember

* Mortuus effe volo, emori nolo.

'right,

'right, is given to *Socrates*: and though it
ftands unexplained by the Author of it, his
Meaning appears to me pretty obvious.
This fagacious Perfon was aware, that we
make our Exits, for the moft Part, under
fome Perturbation or another, if not in a
real Tempeft. His dread therefore of the
Act of dying was very natural: Becaufe a
troublefome Paffage, to an unhofpitable A-
bode, is certainly but an hideous Profpect.
However, he only thought and talked upon
this Occafion, as a Philofopher; whereas I
have my Suggeftions from Defpair. I have
long had, and ftill have, great Reafon to
fear, that my poor fubdued Spirit will leave
me, before I leave the World: And fuch a
Survivance of onefelf, if I may fo call it, is
the greateft of all Calamities. By an un-
accountable Perverfenefs, I have found it at
all Times difproportioned to my Circumftances: For though it was at firft too great
for my Fortune, I feel it now too little for
my Misfortunes. Unlefs I am much de-
ceived, (which frequent Examinations of
myfelf give me little Caufe to fufpect) I was
endued with more than common Temper
and Fortitude: But they have at length for-
faken

faken me: And Hope and Patience, the
Wretch's laft Supports, are fure to join in
fuch a Defertion. " No Man, (as *Brutus*
fays of himfelf) bore Sorrow better : "
But there is a Sorrow not to be borne. A
troubled and refentful Mind, in a diftempered Body, is almoft the Confummation of
human Mifery. And if I have not paft
four and twenty Years in that deplorable
State, may a worfe be allotted me, in fome
future Scene of Exiftence. Lamentable as
fuch a Condition is in itfelf, the Confe-
quences of it were hugely worfe. For when
conftant Watchings, and fome feverer Symp-
toms of my Difeafe, obliged me at length to
have the Advice of a Phyfician ; Doctor *Bur-*
ton, by a moft unheard of Overfight, in
treating my Cafe, which was evidently in-
flammatory, as a nervous one ; told me,
after an Attendance of three Weeks, " that
" my Malady feemed to be in my Mind,
" and he knew of no Medicine, that would
" reach a Grief fo lodged." In confequence
of this fatal Error, if I may be believed, I
paft eleven Years without any more Account
of Time, or other Notices of Things, re-
maining with me, than a Perfon afleep, un-

der

der the Oppreffion of fome horrid Dream.
When he was called again, at the Expiration
of this Term, to a Confultation with another Gentleman of the Faculty, at the Requeft of my invaluable Friend the Bifhop
of *Derry*; he confeffed, that he feared he
had ruined my Health irreparably, and
openly took Shame to himfelf : But, alas !
his Shame was poor Amends for *my* Sorrow.

I doubt, my good and gracious Sir, that
I am making this Appeal to you doubly exceptionable, by adding Melancholy to pro-
lixity : and fhould it affect you at all, it may
poffibly create difagreeable Senfations in you.
But then the Patheticnefs of it befpeaks it
the more genuine ; and that will reconcile
you to it again. I have been told by thofe
about you, that your Abhorrence of every
Thing that is the leaft difingenuous, is a diftinguifhed Part of your Character. If I
have been rightly informed, I fhould con-
clude, that your Majefty would refent a Lie,
juft as another Perfon would a Blow. Yet
when I hear that you are this great Friend
to Truth, I confefs that I confider it only
like any other amicable Attachment: becaufe
Truth

Truth is, and ever will be, a Friend to your
Majesty. She never will seem wanting in
her regard for *You*, till your Historian has
first shewn his disregard for her. He ought
to tell Posterity, that if Lord *Bolingbroke's*
Patriot King has not been exhibited to us;
it was not because the thing itself was not in
your Nature, but because it was not in the
Nature of Things. Neither the Author of
that extravagant Doctrine, " *qui nescit dif-
simulare, nescit regnare ;* " nor *Lewis* the
eleventh, who was such an avowed Favorer
of it, as to say he did not desire his son to
know any more Latin ; could possibly have
convinced me, that your Majesty has been
the worse Ruler, for having never practised
it ; or not the better Man, for having despised
it. He who is false to every-body, will
soon find that he deceives no-body : and
bring at once upon himself the Odium of an
Hypocrite, with the Contempt due to the
Bubble. Indeed and indeed, Sir, the Uni-
versal good Character you bear amongst your
Subjects, added to the early Impressions given
me of you by Lord Carr Hervey, have made
me ever love you, most truly and invariably.
And surely, the Affection of a sincere, honest,
and well endowed Mind, could not but be
deemed

deemed an Acceptable Offering, even to the Deity.——But it is Time to quit this, though for a lefs pleafing Subject, and to tell your Majefty, how infinitely afhamed I fhould be, to fpeak fo inceffantly of myfelf, as I fhall do in this Addrefs to you; were I not avowedly troubling you with it, upon felfifh Motives: and among other, is an ardent Defire I have, if I am to die, not to die wholly unknown to you. As I am about to tell you an uncommon Cafe, your Majefty, I am perfuaded, will forgive my telling it with uncommon Freedom. I fhall have the Confidence even to write to you as my Friend: prefuming, from the noblenefs of your Nature, that you will think it a fufficient Reafon to become fo, to be told I have no other. Hitherto, I have faid very little; but, believe me, I have fuffered abundantly. For great Minds, as I have elfewhere obferved, bear Affliction filently, but they bear it hardly. The Reafon, I believe, is, that the felf-fame Qualities and Affections, which conftitute their greatnefs, are apt, as I conceive, to make them delicate. And delicate Spirits, like delicate Conftitutions, are more liable to little Hurts and Injuries, than thofe

of

of a coarfer Texture. My Conjectures, concerning this fympathetic Union, betwixt greatnefs of Mind, and a *Manly* Softnefs and Senfibility, might be fupported by certain Examples: But your Majefty's Delicacy of another Kind, will probably make you better pleafed with the Omiffion of them.

The adding of Manly to Softnefs, as a Term defcriptive of its Tranfcendency, is, I believe, entirely new. And yet I may venture to affirm, that there is the ftricteft Propriety in it: Becaufe duly confidered, it makes the very Effence of all *Humanity*. The Poet certainly meant to give his Hero an enviable Character, who tells us he had *The gentleft Manners, with the greateft Mind.*

— — And yet, uncommon as this pleafing Affemblage may be, in the component Parts of us; the Thought is fo far from being any Ways ftrained or hyperbolized, that the Behaviour of every Man of Rank and Fafhion, ought at once to give us this Idea of him. Upon a proper Occafion, nothing would fo much exalt or dignify an Hero, in my humble Opinion, as to be found weeping. This Reflection reminds me of an

Oc-

Occurrence, which I fhall take the Liberty
to mention, merely in the Way of Argu-
ment. It happened to me once to be in
waiting on the Queen, at the Time of your
Majefty's Return from *Hanover :* Upon
which Occafion, I faw a very fignal Proof of
what I have hinted at. For, at your firft
Interview with your Family, you was as
much agitated and overborne by the Warmth
and Force of your Affections, as ever any
other Man was by his Paffions. And as
you yourfelf, Sir, have had your Misfortunes, it is a Trouble to me to know, that
he who had Soul enough to feel fuch Emotions from his Joy, muft have at leaft as
quick Senfations, under the Preffure of any
Grief or Adverfity.

But I beg leave to recur to what I was
faying ; becaufe the applying of fuch an
Epithet to myfelf, in any Inftance, may ap-
pear a little arrogant. And to obviate fo
invidious an Imputation, it behoves me to
affure your Majefty, that by greatnefs of
Mind, (in my own Perfon) I meant nothing
more than an enlarged and liberal one ; having been endued from my Youth, with that
Serioufnefs and Simplicity in all my Thoughs
                                    and

and Actions, which I hold fundamentally requifite, to make us both what we wifh, and ought to be. Thus explained and confidered, *my* great Mind will be thought no very great Characteriftic; as it will be found to comprehend little more than Simple Fame. That I have been much too ferious for the World, I have had woeful Experience, by finding the World too little fo for me. It would therefore be cruel to difallow me an Attribute, for which, in the Courfe of a very unhappy Life, I have paid extremely dear. But I have a further View in urging my claim to this Quality; which is, that Serioufnefs and Sincerity being near a-kin, I hope your Majefty will as little doubt of the Singlenefs of my Heart upon this Occafion, as of the other Part of it's Frame and Difpofition.

You will be furprifed to hear, Sir, that when I fat down to write to you, I not only thought I had little to fay to you, but had refolved to fay little: conceiving it would give me a Chance to be the better heard. But the Honour of converfing with you, before I take my final leave of the World, created an unufual Joy in my Heart; and hath awakened the fmall Re-

D   mains

mains of Spirit and Underftanding I havé
about me, to fuch a Degree, that I am under fome Apprehenfion of laying yours a-
fleep. I thought, moreover, as I was about
to afk a Favour of you, that it was incum-
bent on me to give you fome Account of the
Perfon, upon whom you was to confer it :
Of the Truth whereof, I fhall flatter myfelf
that you will not doubt, though the Credit
of the Teftimony, refts fingly upon that of
my Veracity.

Incited by what I tell you, and the very
great Affiance I have in your Majefty's Le-
nity and Goodnefs, I fhall proceed to un-
bofom myfelf to you a little farther. If,
meaning only to be explicit, I feem too co-
pious and diffufe, I have already incurred
your Majefty's Difpleafure by the Length of
my Letter : and now, like an hardened Offender, am perfifting in my Tranfgreffion,
becaufe I think it too late to repent. I have
ftill a longing, methinks, to be known to
you : and partly, from the Confcioufnefs of
what I have loft and fuffered, from not
having had that Honour at my Outfet in the
World. Under the Preffure and Refentment of a Fate like mine, a Man is ever
tormenting himfelf, in his After-thought,
with

with Variety of projected Means for the Avoidance of it. It was but Yefterday, that I was thinking, if my poor dear Brother had been allowed to follicit fome little Employment for me, in the Year Twenty Three, what a Difference it might have made in the whole Courfe of my Fortune. For the Happinefs and Enjoyment of our Lives, depend much more upon little fortuitous Incidents in them, than we are aware. Human Life, in refpect of needy and helplefs Adventurers in it like myfelf, is in effect a Lottery : And an early Eftablifhment in the Court, or a Seat in Parliament, which will pave the way of a Man of Abilities, to the very Sanctum Sanctorum of a Palace, is to have a Ticket in the Wheel at leaft. I am no great Admirer of fententious Writing : but one of *Rouchefocault*'s Obfervations occurs to me, which is fo very appofite to my prefent Purpofe, that I beg leave to quote it. He fays, " *La Nature fait le me-* " *rite, la Fortune le met en Œuvre.*" My Friend Mr. *Legge*, is fuch an Example .of the Truth of this Maxim, as is fcarce parallelled : an Acquaintance with Sir *Edward Walpole*, having fingly determined the Difference, between his having the Guidance

of

of an Helm of a Ship, or his being an
Affiftant at that of the State. Lord *Anfon*
is another Inftance of that Sort : it was his
Voyage round the World, which made him
Lord *Anfon* ; and not the intrinfic Merit of
Captain *Anfon*, great as I am difpofed to allow it, to which he owed his Exaltation.
But as a farther Proof of the Operations of
what we call Luck, in the Affairs of Men ;
that Commiffion and Command, which
were the Foundation of his Power and Dig-
nity, were originally defigned for another
Perfon : And had that Preference taken
Place, the Benignity of his good Genius had
been defeated in the firft Intention ; and the
Ground-work being wanting, the Elevation
could never have been at-all. Neverthelefs, as far as fuch Favourites of this Ideal
Power, have improved Occafions of ad-
vancing or aggrandizing themfelves in the
World, they are greatly to be commended.
For, I think, every Artificer of his own
Fortune, by regular and virtuous Means, is
an Object of Refpect and Admiration. But
not to give up my Author's or my own
Senfe of this matter ; I think I may ftill in-
fift, that the *Terminus a quo*, or Archi-
medes's defired footing, is the main Point *.

Yet

---

* The Gentlemen who have promoted their Fortunes, by
being fent on Embaffies, are numberlefs.

Yet haplefs and hopelefs I, had almoft
reached my End, in vainly looking after
this Beginning. If the conceit I once had
of myfelf, was void of all thofe Deceptions,
to which we are liable from real Self-con-
ceit ; I cannot help thinking, that nothing
but fome propitious Chance, or external Aid
of this Sort, was wanting, to raife me to
fomething more than what I have been. But
your Majefty will be pleafed to obferve, that
the Difference between me and thefe worthy
Gentlemen, is; that your poor forlorn Suitor,
was to feek *his* Fortune, not only without
the ordinary means of looking after it, but
without the leaft Help or Guidance for fuch
a purfuit : whereas, *they* met their appointed
Deftinies, by fo much Accident, and fuch a
concurrence of lucky Circumftances, that
their Fortunes feemed rather to have been
feeking *them*. I flattered myfelf, once or
twice, that I was ftationed for Preferment ;
but ftill my Hopes proved vain. My Situa-
tion was juft like that of the poor Cripple
near the Pool of *Bethefda :* who had neither Powers fufficient of his own to get into
the Bath, nor a tender of any friendly Hand
to do the good Office for him. The politi-
cal Syftem of this Country is fuch, that Gentlemen

tlemen of the moſt diſtinguiſhed Abilities
cannot entirely go alone ; but before I came
into Parliament, my Griefs had ſo utterly
diſqualified me for a Man of Buſineſs, that I
was not able to *move* at-all. And this In-
capacity to ſerve or ſignalize myſelf, added
to the Neglects of thoſe, who could and
ſhould have ſerved me, made the whole
Scene ſo mortifying, that nothing but my
Indigence, (which ought to exclude every
Man from ſuch an Aſſembly) could poſſibly
have tempted me to keep my Seat there ſo
long as I did. If the Chriſtian Doctrines
are founded in Truth and Reaſon, which re-
quire us to do good for Evil ; what Abomi-
nations, both in the ſight of God and Man,
muſt thoſe Creatures be, who return Evil for
Good ? And yet this has been the State of my
Account, with all my principal Relations, on
whom I had any Sort of Dependence.

Though ſuch diſtreſsful Circumſtances,
wanted no Aggravation to make them in-
ſupportable ; it heightened my Reſentment
of them greatly, to find myſelf be-ſet with
almoſt every Evil that could attend an human
Being, unconſcious of having done any thing
to make my Condition worſe than it might
have

have been ; or left undone aught, by which I could hope to mend it. For when I was recalled from *Lincoln's-Inn*, not being above five and twenty Years of Age, (though my Cares had anticipated as many more) I had no fooner obtained my Emancipation from the Dinn and Dirt of the Law, than I made a fecond Attempt, by the Interpofition of my Brother, to prevail on Lord *Briftol*, to purchafe me fome Poft in the Army. But he replied, " I am aftonifhed, Sir, at your " Propofal ; for, by the eternal God, I " would hang him firft." So arbitrary a Rejection of my Suit difmayed me quite. With a Spirit naturally active, and as defirous to fhew itfelf in Action, as ever animated a human Breaft ; I faw myfelf doomed, in confequence of it, to be one of the idle, ufelefs Drones of Society ; and that I fhould live to incur my own Contempt, without having done any thing to incur my own Reproach. But your Majefty fhould know, that this hafty and irrational Anfwer, was meant to convey a Compliment to the over-rated Talents he had conceived in me ; which, upon explaining himfelf, he faid were much too good, to be thrown away in fuch a Calling. By this means, you fee, the

little

little Advantages I was thought to have over some of my Brothers, served but to throw me behind them in the World : these trifling Gifts, by his perverted Sense and misapplication of them, became detrimental to me, in effect : and those very Things, by which others advance themselves so rapidly in life, were given to *me* as reasons, for my not living at-all. You will scarce believe it, Royal Sir; but when my Infirmities, added to some other Reasons I had for taking that Step, obliged me to resign the Employment I had under the good Queen *; I had no other Subsistence whatever for myself and a poor Boy, who has now the honour to be serving You in America, than my fathers dirty Allowance, of one hundred and twenty Pounds a-year. And this poor Pittance, when I called upon him for it, was dealt out to me, with as reluctant an Hand, as he could have paid the Wages of some unfaithful or unprofitable Servant : and as if he looked upon me, rather as an Incumbrance, than a Blessing to him. Upon my Conscience, Sir, I could tell You such enormous

* It was in the Year her Majesty died. I had been her Equerry near nine Years.

things

things of him, as would fill your Mind with
horror; not only as a Man of Probity, but
Humanity. But his Shroud muſt now become a Veil over his Iniquities——That
Peace which he denyed to *me*, be with
him.——

Yet I cannot forbear making one general
Reflection upon the whole; which is, that
as I was deſtined to have a Being, nothing
but the fatallity of deriving it from Lord
Briſtol, could have made me either unhappy, or inconſiderable. I told him often, if
he had any Charge to bring againſt me, and
could ſupport it properly, that I would aſk
his pardon, with all the humility and Sub-
miſſion due to Heaven. But added, that
if ever I forgave what I had to impute to
him, I hoped never to be forgiven myſelf,
where Pardon is of much greater importance
to us. Though I am not entitled to bear
the Motto * of my Family, I feel the
ſubſtance of it internally about me; *for
I never forget.* Inconſiſtent as it may be
with a Religious Orthodoxy, I am even in-
clined to think, that Revenge is one of the

* Je n' oublierai jamais.

E   nenobleft Paffions belonging to our Nature; because it feems to me, to be founded in an Enmity to bafenefs. A very little Attention to the Springs of Action in ourfelves, would convince us, I dare fay, that the felf-fame Spirit which makes our Paffions ftrong, makes our Affections warm : and that we are refentful, and grateful, from homogeneous Principles in us, and an Unity in our Formation. It is my firm belief, at leaft, that he who could foon forget an Injury, would not long remember a good Office.

But although the Law of Retaliation appears to me, to be ftrongly grounded both in Nature and Reafon; yet I faw, as his fon, that I was precluded all Power and Means of making any Reprifals upon him whatever. The only fatisfaction, therefore, that remained, for all his inhuman Injuries, was, to mortify his Pride as well as I could : Where, as he was moft fenfible, I knew, of courfe, that he was moft vulnerable. Accordingly, I boldly afferted at one Time, that I owed him nothing but a Being, which he feemed to have ftudied how to make burthenfom and loathfom to me. I told him at another, in a more dejected Mood, that,

had

had he not made a Wretch, I might poffibly have excufed his making *nothing* of me ;
and would have compounded with him, for
depriving me of all other Enjoyments, if he
would but have allowed me to enjoy myfelf.
For Neglects, as I obferved to him, are but
negative Wrongs ; and hold no Proportion,
or Comparifon, with abfolute Injuries and
Abufes.   With thefe and the like Re-
proaches, occafionally inferted in my Letters to him, would he fuffer me to fting his
Confcience, and gall his Pride, without the
leaft Reply, Gainfaying, or Recrimination
whatever.   Strange Man ! or rather ftrange
Monfter! for I am thoroughly perfuaded,
that fuch a Creature never appeared before
in an human Shape.

I believe he loved me once, as well as he
could love, but not fo well as I could have
wifhed.   For, being never actuated by any
real Principle, his Affections were nothing
more than conftitutional Emotions, occafionally excited in him, like the Compaffion
of another Perfon, when he gives his Alms
to a Beggar : All Pity creating for a while,
a certain Degree of Love of its Object.
But from the Time that my Mother con-

victed him, before my Face, and in the
Prefence of Lord Chief Baron *Reynolds*,
(whom fhe did not entirely acquit of being
privy to the Collufion) of having defrauded
me of twelve hundred Pounds a-year, he
feemed difconcerted always, and uneafy at
the Sight of me. The Relation betwixt
Caufe and Effect, with regard to this dia-
bolic Kind of Enmity, is fomewhat occult;
but I believe it may be taken for granted,
that almoft every Man hates the Perfon,
whom he has greatly and wilfully injured.
I think I could give a tolerable Account of
the Ground and Growth of it, but the Ana-
lyfis would be too tedious.

That he had wondrous Reafon to regard
me, God knows! For I call the fame Judge
to witnefs, whether the Love and Reve-
rence I once bore him, did not furpafs every
thing of its Kind in this World, excepting
that of the Religious for himfelf. But all
the Ufe my Tyrant made of this extraordinary Refpect and Deference, was to take
Advantage of an eafy generous Nature, and
make it acceffary to my own Undoing. For
from the Time that he obtained, I may fay
extorted from me, my Confent to be made

a Member of the Corporation of *Bury*, I may date the moft material Evils, that have attended my wretched Life. My good and gracious Sir, I not only facrificed my Time and Health in performing the irkfome, flavifh Offices he impofed upon me there; but, what is fcarce credible, I did them at my own Expence. When I wanted to make a little Merit of thefe Services with my Brother, who at that Time reaped the Benefit of my Drudgery, I did not find him difpofed to treat me much better than my Parents. And in a Conference I had with him fome Time after, upon another Occafion, he behaved himfelf with fuch unfufferable Arrogance, that I broke off all Intercourfe and Commerce with him, for almoft four Years.

A barely flighted Friendfhip, Sir, is a mortifying Thing enough; but an abufed and ill-requited Love, is a fhocking one. But my Brother's Mif-ufage, though it helped to produce a dreadful Change in me, did not change my Purpofes. I have returned to my Toil, with the fame Zeal and Fervour, and embarked a-new, for the fake of his Children, in what I thought a very meritorious

torious Undertaking. For I fhall ever love
my Family, as I do my Country, collec-
tively; though I may have feen Caufe to
defpife Individuals of both.

I moft humbly befeech You, my good
and gracious Sovereign, to pardon the un-
wary Trefpafs I have comitted, in extending
thefe Reflections to fo great a length, after
feeming to have difmifs'd the horrid Subject.
But, upon my word, it poffeffes my whole
Soul in fuch a manner, that whenever I
touch upon it, I fcarce poffefs myfelf. To
find out that we have been the Dupes of our
own Hearts; which is the cafe of every Man,
who lives to difcover that he has been the
Friend of his Enemy; is attended with
fuch a deadly Anguifh, as none will ever
know, but thofe who have felt it: And
is never to be defcribed, even by them that
have. I beg leave, neverthelefs, to make
known to Your Majefty one more untoward
Circumftance, attending this fatal Occupa-
tion affigned me by my Father, and fhall fo
conciude.

Lady Briftol, having been highly difobli-
ged by my Colleague at Bury, who was
likewife growing very unpopular there; told

me

me one Day, that she was resolved to seek
Revenge, by supplanting him in the Borough.
That her Confederates in this Design, having numbered the Malcontents, had assured
her upon the last Muster of them, they were
strong enough to effect it ; and, if I either
voted for him, or took any Measures for
the farther Support of his Interest in the
Corporation, that I should repent it as long
as I lived.   In short, if I did any Thing to
defeat her Project, that she would strike
me out of her Will.   The Purport of my
Answer, which I do not pretend to give
your Majesty with great Exactness, was ;
that I was very much concerned, and a little surprised, at this new Difficulty she had
thrown in my Way.   Colonel *Norton*, I
confessed, was a Person, whom I had no
Reason to love, had some to distrust, and
many to despise.   But I reminded her La-
dyship, at the same Time, of a proverbial
Maxim, which imports, that there is an
Equity due to the Devil : and told her farther, as it appeared to me to have some
Foundation in Reason, I had resolved to
act conformably to it.   That in Pursuance
of this Resolution, in the last Conference I
had

had with my Father, (though, in my own private Opinion, I thought all Coalitions injurious to his Intereſt) I had ſet forth the Expediency of ſupporting the preſent one ; and, as the Alliance was ſubſiſting, that the Stipulations and Obligations of it ſurely were to be obſerved. His Lordſhip, I told her, having approved of theſe and other Arguments I uſed, of the ſame Tendency, impowered me to tell the Confederate Party, that in order to ſtrengthen their Hands, he ſhould acquieſce in the Choice of the two Perſons, whom they had propoſed to him for that Purpoſe. " And you have done all " this, have you ? (replied her Ladyſhip) " then You have acted the Part of a Scoun- " drel, *for* a Scoundrel." This outrageous Violence ſeeming to exceed all Authority or Licenſe claimable by any Parent, though incenſed, I remained at Table but juſt Time enough to hear her Menaces reiterated, and withdrew *. But her Ladyſhip's Impetuoſity upon this Occaſion, unfortunately be-

* This curious Converſation paſt in the Preſence of two or three Perſons who had dined wirh her that Day, her Ladyſhip being then at *Tunbridge.Wells.*

trayed

trayed my poor double-dealing Father; who, as appeared, had it not been for my feasonable Inftigation, was to have connived at her Device. But the Iffue of our Conflict, my good Sir, was worfe than the Thing itfelf; for when fhe died, I found that I had fuffered the Penalty denounced againft me, for my unpardonable Offence. Though my Mother, as your Majefty knows, was a very weak and paffionate Woman; it is my Opinion, that her Wrath would not have carried her fuch a Length, unfomented by fome indirect Practices of another Relation of mine. At the fame Time, I think myfelf bound to confefs, that this Allegation is grounded chiefly on Surmife; and that Charges of fo heinous a Nature, ought to have more than prefumptive Proofs to fupport them. It is certain, however, that he whom I fufpect, was the Perfon benefitted by our unhappy Quarrel. But be it, or be it not, aggravated, with the Bafenefs fuppofed; the Cruelty of the Proceeding is fo glaring, that it is needlefs to defire your particular Attention to it: One of my Parents having exacted from me the moft fevere Services, that ever were required of a

F   Son;

Son ; and the other difinherited me for the
Performance of them. It is not neceffary
to *fuffer* fuch things as thefe, Royal Sir ;
to hear of them is fufficient to make us Melancholy. Relationfhip feems to me, to be
one of the Conjunctions disjunctive: And
nothing can more plainly fhew the Degene-
racy of Mankind, than that the Ties of Blood,
by fome Means or another, prove much of-
tener the Caufes of Strife and Envy, than
the Bands of Amity in Families.

I had almoft forgot to tell you, by a
ftrange Occurrence of my Life, it happened
to me, that your Majefty's Intereft once in-
terfered with mine : But I thank Heaven,
that I had Grace and Refolution enough to
give yours the Preference. And I do moft
folemnly proteft to you, my ever loved and
honoured Mafter, that when I have
been engaged in what I thought right, I
never could be awed by the Apprehenfion,
either of Danger, Difficulty, or Lofs, that
might attend the Performance of it. This
Inflexibility, I believe, is always the Con-
commitant of a proud and dedignant Spirit :
And though the Qualities may not feem
pleafing, I wifh the Character was more
com-

common. Pride that will not let a Man
bend his Back properly, is offenſive and con-
temptible : but Pride that will not let him
bend to *Things*, improperly, is of ſo glo-
rious a Nature, that he may even be proud
of his pride.

To conſummate my Affliction, I have
lately diſcovered, that this little Fort in my
Formation, was, pretty near, all that the
cenſorious World had allowed or left me now
to brag of. I have been informed by a very
ſincere and faithful Friend of mine, (and
none are faithful that are not as ſincere) that
my Character and Conduct have not eſcaped
Cenſure and Deriſion. And, in Truth, Sir,
I have been unhappily aware, that the con-
ſtant Violences I have been doing to myſelf, in conſequence of the Outrages done
me by others, could not but expoſe me to
ſuch invidious Comments and Animadver-
ſions. Inclination, and Deſperation, make
very different Men frequent the ſame Paths,
and affect the ſame Haunts and Habits ; and
the By-ſtander, who cannot poſſibly diſcern
the various Cauſes of their Attraction, naturally
brings us both under the ſame Predicament.
By which Means, we become injured, with-

F 2   out

out having any thing, in reallity, to impute to the Doer of the Wrong. It is a Misfortune, that we have no other way to judge of what paffes in the World, but by Appearances, or Report, And yet how very few things, are either what they feem, or are reprefented to be? I can teftify, that I have often feen a Philofopher, affimilate himfelf, and become the Companion of an empty Sot. I have feen, at other times, Perfons of moft diftinguifhed Honour and good Senfe, promifcuoufly met, and levelled, with a noify diffolute Tribe of another Sort; and yet having no more real Call to the Object of their Attention, than they would have had, any where elfe, to their Society. A *tædium fui*, I doubt, Sir, is too commonly the Source of Vice, amongft the Idle and Indolent: but that *tædium* in a Wretch, to whom the Joys of a felf-poffeffing, and felf-applauding Mind, had been ever known, becomes an Impulfe of a very different Nature. What I mean to point out by thefe Remarks, is, that the Characters of Gentlemen are not to be determined by the Purfuit of the fame Pleafures. For fome will be feen to follow them, merely becaufe they like them; whilft
others

others may be found to feek them, only becaufe they *diflike* themfelves.   What I could
fay more upon this Subject, I hope will be
fupplied, by your Majefty's candid Application of what I have faid.   For to have our
Misfortunes, or the Effects of them, turned
to our Reproach, is a moft lamentable En-
hancement of .them.   The Truth is, my
good and gracious Sovereign, that my whole
Life has been fpent, as it were, in a Storm.
And I have always feared, that the miftaken
World, who have beheld my Wreck, would
lay the blame upon the poor Owner of the
Veffel, inftead of giving it to the carelefs
and unthinking Pilot, who fhould have fhewn
me a better Courfe.

I have troubled You, Sir, with a very tedious Rhapfody ; and, inftead of recommending to your Confideration a Cafe only,
which was all I promifed in the Introduc-
tion to it, perceive that I have infenfibly
become my own Biographer.   However,
the enormous Length of my Performance ex-
cepted, I flatter myfelf, that it contains
nothing at-all offenfive, either in point of
Manner, or Matter.   If, in fetting forth
any thing, which I thought praife-worthy

in

in my Conduct, there has appeared a little
femblance of Oftentation; as I am moft un-
feignedly confcious, that it was not from
any vain or arrogant Motive, I hope it will
not be imputed to me as a Breach of Mo-
defty. For I can aver, with the ftricteft
Regard to Truth, that I pretend to no other
Merit now in this World, than that of having deferved a bettet Fate and Treatment in
it.

I am convinced, that I have written fuch
a Letter to your Majefty, as was never before addreffed to any King. But then it
contains a Story too, which no Subject but
myfelf ever had to write : And You are the
only Perfon on Earth, to whom I would
condefcend to tell it. It is little Evils (fays a
Latin Aphorifm) which difpofe us to com-
plain; but great ones make us ftupid, and
fpeechlefs *. I have ftifled my Griefs, till
I have fometimes thought, that they would
ftifie *me*. For Pity is a Boon, which my
Temper would never allow me to feek, nor
my Experience to expect. It feems to me,
at beft, to be but a kind of mental Charity ;

* Curæ leves loquuntur, ingentes ftupent.

and

and Men of Spirit can but ill brook, the standing indebted for such Alms.

Approaching very nearly, now, the End of *my* Pleasure, and your Majesty's Pains; which could not have been compatible, in any other Instance; I am reminded by it, of an humorous Observation of Lord Verulam's, who remarks of some of the Epistolary Writers in his Time, that it was their constant Practice, to make the Postscript, the most material Part of their Letters. For, somewhat like these Gentlemen, I have reserved for the last Article of my Remonstrance, that which I originally designed for the whole Sum and Substance of it.

It is most humbly to represent to your Majesty, that I have had a Demand upon your Treasury, of a Civil-list Arrear of long standing, to the Amount of two thousand Pounds. Encouraged by my Friends, I found Means to make known this Claim to Mr. *Pelham*; who acknowledged the Validity of it, and assured me it should be complied with. Some Months after my first Application, pursuant to his Desire, I renewed my Petition, and he his Promise, that he would not forget his Engagement. But seeing
ing

ing him frequently, and no Mention being made of it, I dropt my Suit. This Debt accrued, Sir, in the Manner following. Sir *Robert Walpole*, after numberlefs Profeffions of his Love, and Regard for me, told me at his Levee one Morning, that your Majefty had at laft enabled him to give me a more fubftantial Proof of them, by appointing me one of your Clerks of the Green-Cloth. Having poftponed me often, to thofe I fhould have preceeded, by his own Confeffion ; his general Pretence for neglecting me had been, that I had neglected myfelf, by being a bad Sollicitor. And it is very true, that I never was, what is called, in modern and modifh Phrafe, a pufhing Man : though the Urgency of my Wants, might have excufed a little Appearance of it, in the Manner of my defiring to have them fupplied. However, the good Office he had done me with'your Majefty, atoned for every thing. When I had been about a Week, as I thought, in Poffeffion of this Employment, and expecting daily to be called to the Acknowledgment of your Bounty, as is cuftomary, by having the honour to kifs your Hand ; I waited upon him again, in order to be informed, whether

any

any Time was fixed for that Purpofe. But
he told me, to my great Surprife, and Concern, that he feared the Duke of *Dorfet*,
who had folicited the Office for Mr. *Carew*,
would get the better of me. That his
Grace having two or three Sons in Parliament, had threatened him, if he could not
carry his Point, with the entire Defection
of his whole Family. The demur was fufficient to convince me, what would be the
refult of our Competition ; and I was obliged
to acquiefce under another Difappointment.
But I received a Meffage from him not long
after, fignifying that he defired to fpeak with
me; and at this Interview, he made me an
Offer of the Place I enjoy at prefent under
your Majefty ; which I abfolutely refufed.
Sir *Robert*, notwithftanding, being himfelf
diffatisfied, with the Slight he had put upon
me ; I had a fecond Meffage from him, conveyed to me by the then Bifhop of *Ely*, who
was my particular friend. This Commiffion
was to inform me, that your Majefty, in
order to make the Employment I had refufed, more equivalent to that which I had
loft ; had impowered him to give it me,

G

with

with an additional Salary of Four Hundred Pounds a-Year; till you could provide for me, as he was pleafed to fay, more fuitably to my Defert. Little expecting to meet, and much lefs able to bear any new Diftrefs or Mortification, I am almoft afhamed to tell You, that your Proxy upon this Occa-fion, neither paid my fupplemental Ap-pointments, nor ever procured me any other Mark of your Favour, in Lieu of them. The Ufe I hope to make of the Non-Per-formance of this Agreement, is rather as an Interceffor for my poor Family, than as a Principal. An Acceffion to my Fortune, upon the Death of Sir *Thomas Hanmer*, having made my Income compleatly Two Thoufand Pounds a-Year, I have thought myfelf, ever fince, as rich as your Majefty*. For, I am not one of thofe very fine Gentle-men, in the Eftimate of whofe Expences, Superfluities feem to be become a confider-able Part of their Neceffaries.

But although I have no immediate Wants of my own; Attention to the future Wel-fare of thofe I ought to hold dear as myfelf, is a concern not inferiour to any other whatever.

---

* A nominal two thoufand Pounds a-year is here meant; whereof my Salary made one Quarter.

ever. And it is fingly with this View, that I have taken the Liberty to remind your Majefty of your intended Benefaction to me. Let me intreat You, therefore, as there may be fhortly an End of *me*, to allow me the Satisfaction, of feeing firft an End of thofe Things, that, in all Likelihood, have prematurely brought me to it; and not to fuffer my Child, or his Mother, to be Heirs to my Griefs, who, if I die foon, may have little elfe to inherit.

It was ever my fincere Opinion, that the moft enviable of all human Happinefs, is the Power of making happy. And though the want of the Power, has left me alfo in want of the Proof of my Propofition; I am luckily applying myfelf, to the Perfon in the World beft qualified, both by Nature and Habit, to confirm the Truth of it. A Man, I dare fay, has but to make out a very moderate Title to your Beneficence, to do you a reciprocal Pleafure in the be-ftowing of it. For which Reafon, if I fucceed not in my prefent Purpofe, I fhall attribute the Mifcarriage to an Infufficiency

G 2

in

in my Claim, and not to any Defect in the Difpofition of my Patron.

Having apprifed your Majefty, long fince, of my End in writing to you ; I hope, and truft, that you will pardon me, if I prefume to tell you likewife, by what Means you may moft effectually anfwer it. And, that your Majefty's good Intentions towards me, may not be entirely defeated ; I humbly propofe, in the way of Commutation, that you will now permit my Wife to reap the Benefit of them, by giving her a Penfion of two hundred Pounds a-year. Or, fhould your Confideration of thirty Years Services, and the many difagreeable Things I encountered in the Performance of my Duty, incline you to a more generous Requital of them ; you may make me ftill happier, in beftowing on my Son, the Employment I have the Honour to hold of you. And to obviate any Scruples you may have about multiplying of Reverfions, I am not only willing, but defirous, in Confideration of fo great a Favour, to relinquifh my own Intereft in it, entirely. Should your Majefty be gracioufly pleafed

to

to indulge my Suit, by this Method of complying with it; you will not barely difcharge your Debt, but, in fact, transfer the Credit to your own Side, by an accumulated Bounty; and without miffing the Means of doing either. And this great End and Aim of all my Wifhes, accomplifhed; I fhall withdraw myfelf, as far as is confiftent with Mrs. *Hervey*'s Pleafures, from a disjointed, envious, and diffolute World, with which I have long been jangling; and of which I fhall take my final Leave, with as much Unconcern, as I could turn my Back upon any other Spectacle, where I had neither liked the Reprefentation, nor the Performers. One of the melancholy Comforts of a Life of Difcontent, is, that it brings Content in Death. And though the Lofs of it, profpectively confidered, is accounted the greateft Evil that can befall us; yet, confequentially regarded, it is the leaft : Becaufe it is a Lofs, of which we have no Senfe. Having done fome Things I may be proud of, and none to be afhamed of, I fhall footh and folace myfelf with thofe Thoughts; and acquiefce

in

in the pleafing Recognition of them, 'till my appointed Hour fhall come, in which nothing but fuch a Confcioufnefs is of any Moment to us. And during the tedious Interval, I fhall fecretly pray Heaven, a-mongft other Supplications for your Well-being; that you may be juft as long-lived as you wifh yourfelf, as happy as I wifh you, and as much beloved as you deferve.

I have the Honour to be, with a moft unfeigned and unutterable Devotion,

Your Majefty's

ever faithful and

Bond-ftreet
Feb. 3, 1755.
obedient humble Servant,

Thomas Hervey.

F I N I S.

www.ingramcontent.com/pod-product-compliance
Lightning Source LLC
Chambersburg PA
CBHW022026080426
42733CB00007B/739